MANAGING BEHAVIOUR

A PRACTICAL FRAMEWORK FOR SCHOOLS

New Edition

Sheila Wolfendale and Trevor Bryans

A NASEN PUBLICATION

ISBN 0 906730 59 7

Published by NASEN Enterprises Ltd.
NASEN Enterprises is a company limited by guarantee, registered in England and Wales. Company No. 2637438.

Further copies of this book and details of NASEN's many other publications may be obtained from the Publications Department at its registered office:
2 Lichfield Road, Stafford ST17 4JX (Tel: 0785 46872 Fax: 0785 41187)

Cover design by Pam Crewe.
Typeset in Palatino and printed in the United Kingdom by Impress Printers (Stoke-on-Trent) Ltd. Tel: 0782 287677

MANAGING BEHAVIOUR

Contents

Preface

This new edition of *Managing Behaviour* has been updated to include the impact and effects of recent and new legislation as well as developments which have ensued as a result of the Elton Report (1989). This influential government report has focussed public and political attention on the issue of children who behave badly in school *(Choice and Diversity, 1992,* p 11, para. 1.54 and the *Education Act, 1993).* Educational legislation now provides a statutory framework for schools to adopt policies on discipline and behaviour management, as well as having to be accountable for these to governors, parents and inspection teams *(Education (Schools) Act, 1992; Framework for Inspection, 1993).*

Under Section 157 of the *Education Act 1993,* the Secretary of State for Education will issue from time to time (beginning September 1994), a Code of Practice giving guidance to LEAs and the governing bodies of all maintained schools on the discharge of their functions under Part III of the Act towards all children with special educational needs. LEAs and governing bodies *must* have regard to the provisions of the Code. The Code recognises that there is a continuum of special educational needs and offers practical guidance to schools and LEAs on the identification of *all* pupils with special educational needs (SEN), advocating the general adoption of a staged model of assessment. It contains criteria for the making of statutory assessments and statements, guidance on the procedures to be adopted and guidance on the conduct of annual reviews.

We make reference, particularly in Sections 5, 6 and 7 to the requirements of the Code, and particularly to the forging of new partnerships between all those concerned with the SEN pupils in schools.

The Code of Practice identifies the main SEN areas, one of which is **Emotional and Behaviour Difficulties** (set out in Stage 3). Here, the explicit link between emotional and behaviour difficulties and failure to achieve in school is made so that schools must have clear recorded evidence of both the child's academic attainment and the nature of his or her problems.

In January 1994 the Department for Education issued a number of draft circulars for consultation, with the intention of these coming into practice during 1994. Of these, several are directly concerned with behaviour and discipline. They are : Pupil Behaviour and Discipline; the Education of Children with Emotional and Behavioural Difficulties; Exclusions from School. These draft circulars give evidence on the responsibilities of head teachers and governing bodies as to the management

4

of pupil behaviour in schools. Building upon the recommendations of the Elton Report, they encourage schools to have policies on bullying, sanctions, exclusions and parental involvement in these issues, as well as schools' partnership with key support services, in particular the educational psychology service.

Schools are now in charge of, and have control over, their own finances and, consequently, are responsible for their own provision. Nevertheless, in broad terms, special educational needs issues and resourcing remain a collective responsibility, wherein locally supplied support staff still exist to offer expertise and help to individual schools.

The basic premise of this book is that the teacher is directly and responsibly concerned with the social and emotional development of children in her/his charge. A framework is proposed in the book to enable teachers to re-examine their attitudes and develop a range of responsive and effective strategies within a supportive framework of collective responsibility.

This new edition has several purposes:

1. to extend the theoretical scope of the earlier booklet by incorporating contemporary perspectives;

2. to refer to the considerable number of innovative and practical programmes designed to deal with disruptive behaviour and to promote effective learning;

3. to make accessible a range of strategies and approaches, and to provide suggestions for further reading;

4. to provide a starting point for planning in-service training for staff;

5. to convey the necessity for schools to develop whole-school policies in this area, and for teachers to acknowledge and respond positively to diversity within our schools.

We envisage that this book can be used in the following ways:

- as a source of stimulus material;
- as a basis for programme design in schools;
- as a facilitator for school or centrally-focussed in-service training.

Managing Behaviour is intended for teachers, governors, non-teaching and support staff across the age range, from pre-school to secondary education settings. It is divided into a number of sections each of which follows a similar format: introduction and a discussion of the issues - which are predominantly practically focussed - followed by a list of further reading. This list of texts combines background theory with useful ideas and suggestions to try out.

In this edition, Section 8, now called 'A Treasury', has been considerably revised and extended, to give more information on materials for professional development courses and bullying, now acknowledged to be a major area of concern. All the referenced material in this edition has been carefully selected to ensure contemporary relevance, whilst retaining seminal influences.

References
Choice and Diversity (1992), HMSO: London.

Code of Practice and Regulations on the Identification of Pupils with Special Educational Needs, Regulations on Assessments and Statements (1994) HMSO: London.

Education Acts
Education (Schools) Act (1992), HMSO: London.

Education Act (1993), HMSO: London.

Elton Report (1989), *Discipline in Schools,* HMSO: London.

Framework for Inspection (1993) (2nd Edition), OFSTED: London.

OFSTED (1993), *Achieving Good Behaviour in Schools,* HMSO: London.

Section 1 - Troubling and Troublesome Behaviour : a Rationale

Explanatory frameworks for troubling and troublesome behaviour have been elaborated and expanded over the past few years, from individual pathology to analyses of school and classroom practices and social interaction.

The synonymous and alternative use of labels to describe 'deviant', 'antisocial', 'disturbed' behaviour and the formal substitution in many places of the term 'maladjusted' by 'emotionally and behaviourally disturbed' and, latterly, by the terms 'disaffected' and 'challenging behaviour' may only mask the perennial issues confronting teachers. That is to say, they face the dichotomy of, on the one hand having to retain control and, on the other, needing to be responsive and sensitive to the distress experienced by some children. The particular dilemma arises when individual stress manifests itself in direct confrontational and conflict situations that threaten control and classroom order: a totally stressful predicament for the teacher as well as the child.

Nowadays, many programmes and approaches exist to assist and support teachers in coping with incidents and issues of classroom control, as well as helping them to respond to the need to effect behaviour change for the better in individual children. The rest of this book aims to provide a review of current thinking and available approaches across the range of relevant classroom practices.

The book may serve as a stimulus for reappraisal of attitudes and practices towards troubling and troublesome behaviour, including inappropriate learning habits. Whilst the literature on disruptive and inappropriate learning behaviour goes back many years, it is only recently that there has been critical scrutiny of attitudes, contexts and actions that define and shape pupils' behaviour. Furthermore, irrespective of pupils presenting problems of behaviour, they are all entitled to full access to the National Curriculum. So the challenge for teachers is thus to differentiate for all pupils, taking their personal and social needs into account. Research suggests that this balance is achievable. As the following extract from Cooper (1993) outlines:

> '...it can be said that research shows that teachers in effective mainstream schools relate to their pupils in ways which stress their positive regard for pupils. There is a clear sense of continuity between the interpersonal and social relationships throughout the school. When teachers relate to whole groups of pupils, they are taking careful account of the individual differences among their pupils and catering for these. Where pupils require individual

attention, teachers make efforts to make themselves available to pupils. Such teachers are also more likely to set up patterns of classroom interaction that encourage pupils to participate and thus display their interests and capabilities. Teachers also communicate their positive regard for pupils through the use of praise and by creating conditions in the classroom that help to encourage pupils to perform well. Such conditions include the quality of the learning environment which, in effective schools, often gives the impression of being cared for as well as being educationally stimulating'. (pp 175-6)

A Societal View

Professed concern by the media, by parents as well as by educationalists and the Government as to the incidence of violent acts and reported lack of discipline, has acted as a constructive focus for reappraisal of:

- the initial training of teachers in handling individuals and groups;
- how teachers are assisted and supported in organising and managing learning environments of all kinds;
- how pupils themselves and their parents can be effectively included in the equation;
- the extent to which schools need to review and revise their discipline and sanction systems, together with their pastoral care provision.

In response to such public concern, the Government set up an enquiry into discipline in schools. The Committee, chaired by Lord Elton, was asked to consider what action could be taken by all concerned - the Government, local authorities, school governors, teachers and parents - 'to secure the orderly atmosphere necessary in schools for effective teaching and learning to take place'.

There is a consensus across the political divides: responsibility for securing the 'orderly atmosphere' is collective. This principle is embedded, in a broader sense, within the provisions of the *Education Reform Act 1988*. However, the landscape has changed. With a percentage of schools now grant-maintained and with all schools in charge of their own budgets, there is a danger of this principle of collective responsibility being eroded within a climate of decentralisation and local authorities no longer equipped to encourage an overall, across-authority policy and practice.

It is imperative, therefore, to set up new alliances within and among schools for sharing practice and support structures to enable effective teaching and learning to occur.

Summary of the main conclusions and recommendations of the Elton Report (1989)

Incidents of physical threat or violence towards teachers are relatively rare, but teachers reported, in the survey commissioned by the Elton Committee, that they experience considerable and recurring stress as a result of the permanent vigilance needed to manage pupils. The survey also confirmed the evident link between under-achievement and disaffected behaviour. The Report also acknowledged that teacher training institutions paid scant attention to issues of classroom management, so newly-trained teachers feel ill-equipped and unprepared to cope with the 'continuous stream of minor disruptions'.

Essentially, the Elton Report provides in its collection of recommendations the basis for coherent policies on behaviour management, discipline and pastoral systems. Below we highlight and paraphrase a number of these recommendations which are directed to LEAs, schools, pupils and parents.

LEAs:
- should set up systems to monitor disruptions;
- should provide in-service training and support, using appropriate available materials and methods.

Schools and Governors:
- should draw up 'clear statements on behaviour', with a balance between rewards and punishment and consistent distinctions between minor and serious offences;
- should promote a positive atmosphere for all pupils 'regardless of ability and aptitude'.

Pupils:
- should be encouraged to participate directly via, for example, Records of Achievement;
- should be consulted by their teachers on matters of school policy to do with behaviour management in schools.

Parents:
- should be urged to take greater direct responsibility for their children's behaviour in general;
- should co-operate with schools in implementing school systems of behaviour management.

The impact and effects of the Elton Report

- It has been a useful lever and reference point and has served to place the issue of disruption firmly onto the educational agenda.
- It has been a means of securing and generating central and local funds for provision of in-service and school-focussed training, via GEST (Grants for Educational Support and Training) and the Education Support Grant.
- It has been a starting point for re-appraisal of school-based practice, including the setting of whole school policies on discipline and behaviour management.
- It has been a stimulus for developing local and nationally available materials to support teachers' in-service education (see Section 8).
- It has provided a means for promoting inter-professional working links, for example, between teachers and welfare assistants.

Further reading

These selected references are recommended to readers wishing to follow up these areas:

- definitions of, and attitudes to, disruptive behaviour;
- principles, practice and provision;
- collective responsibility;
- reviews of recent literature;
- ecological perspectives;
- disruptive behaviour in the early years.

Booth, T and Coulby, D (Eds) (1987) *Producing and Reducing Disaffection: Curricula for All,* Open University Press: Milton Keynes.

Cohen, L and Cohen, D (Eds) (1987) *Disruptive Behaviour: A Source Book for Teachers,* Harper and Row: London.

Elton, Lord (Chairman) (1989) *Discipline in Schools: Report of the Committee of Enquiry,* HMSO: London.

Cooper, P (1993) *Effective Schools for Disaffected Students,* Routledge: London.

Lennox, D (1991) *See Me After School,* David Fulton Publishers: London.

Richman, N and Lansdowne, R (Eds) (1988) *Problems of Pre-School Children,* (chaps. 9 & 10), John Wiley: Chichester.

Tattum, D (Ed) (1986) *Management of Disruptive Pupil Behaviour in Schools*, John Wiley: Chichester.

Thomas, G and Feiler, A (Eds) (1988) *Planning for Special Needs: A Whole School Approach*, Simon and Schuster: London.

Wolfendale, S (1992) 'The Management of Behaviour in School', in Wolfendale, S. *Primary Schools and Special Needs: policy, planning and provision* (2nd edition). Cassell: London.

Section 2 - Identifying Problem Behaviour

In general, a pupil or young person is thought to have behaviour difficulties if there is evidence of disruption to everyday activity, school or college functioning.

Emotional and behaviour problems can usually be distinguished from:

- specific learning difficulties;
- general learning difficulties;
- physical conditions;
- the effects of social disadvantage.

Many children with overt 'reactive' behaviour problems quickly come to the notice of teachers. Yet there are large numbers of pupils whose difficulties are not immediately apparent or visible in school. These include bullied or abused children, and children with such a generalised lack of self-esteem that they underfunction, unnoticed, in all areas.

Pupils with emotional or behavioural problems also evince difficulties in some or all of these other areas, and teachers are familiar with this pattern. However, these difficulties may only be in evidence at school, not at home or in other social settings - so the use of a 'blanket' label in referring to a child as 'maladjusted', 'disruptive' or 'learning disabled' is not appropriate or helpful.

Learning and behaviour problems are usually age-norm related, such that behaviour which is acceptable at one age is not at another. Below are listed groups of more common behaviour difficulties by age occurrence:

Pre-school (aged 2-5)
- sleeping and eating problems;
- disobedience, aggression, temper tantrums;
- hyperactivity, severe restlessness, poor concentration;
- slow language development.

Mid-childhood (aged 6-12)
- conduct problems: aggression, disobedience, truancy;
- emotional problems: misery, depression, anxiety;
- poor general progress at school, reading and writing difficulties.

Adolescent (aged about 13 to 17)
- conduct problems: delinquency, truancy, defiance, aggression;
- depression, anxiety states, phobias, school refusal;
- disaffection with school or college, poor academic achievement.

A number of key issues connected with learning and behaviour problems need to be highlighted for consideration:

- Learning and behaviour problems are rarely self-reported in the first instance, but are interpreted in various contexts by parents, teachers, doctors, psychologists and other professions, most of whom use their own value systems and professional backgrounds to do this.
- Parents and teachers particularly differ in their definitions and perceptions of childhood problems and their causes.
- Cause and effect are notoriously difficult to disentangle at various ages in a child's life.
- Boys tend to exhibit more 'acting out' behaviour than girls, by about two and a half times.
- Girls show more fear than boys.
- Whatever the real cause of origin of a learning or behaviour problem, it will often manifest itself elsewhere, e.g. distress or stress at home will sometimes show in disruptive behaviour at school. Equally, negative experiences at school may result in inappropriate behaviour at home.
- At secondary level, increasing numbers of pupils display behavioural signs consistent with substance abuse and addiction (alcohol and/or drugs).
- It is the context in which the problems occur that ways and means of ameliorating the difficulties need to be found.
- Many children and young people exhibit emotional or behaviour problems of one sort or another. In fact, probably the majority in passing from infancy to adulthood have done so. Most of these problems are temporary and do not require detailed diagnosis and follow-up intervention, because they are related to life changes in the family or domestic routine, change of school or peer group.
- Emotional and behaviour problems, as well as learning difficulties, are more significant if they persist or become worse over time.
- In general, it is true that conduct disorders such as aggression, stealing or delinquency are more difficult to deal with than neurotic behaviour such as phobias or fears.

This list is, of course, not exhaustive. (See also Lennox (1991) and Rutter and Rutter (1992).

At many points throughout this book the emphasis on how and why behaviour problems emerge in any setting is shifted towards the teacher or primary carer. Teachers' behaviour and attitudes are crucial in minimizing the occurrence of inappropriate behaviour in the first place, and in ensuring continued low evidence of such problems at school. Therefore, all interventions must include a careful consideration of the influence of teachers' reactions in lessening or, perhaps, increasing the inappropriate behaviour.

Overt, 'acting-out' behaviour
Recognition and assessment

The main purpose of assessment is to focus the observer's attention on the whole child as well as on positive and negative features of a child's behaviour so that an accurate picture of what the child actually does, how frequently, and in what situations, can be produced. In other words, objective observation defines the behaviour and its associated problems to be tackled. Most forms of assessment require direct knowledge of the child in question, and usually offer some scope, in the completion of a check list or scale, for extra comments to be recorded. Only when an accurate record of the child's behaviour has been made can a programme of behaviour change be initiated. We need to know: what happens, when, how often, in whose company, and in what circumstances.

A framework to describe and record behaviour used in behavioural psychology is the A-B-C model, in which A is *antecedent* behaviour (prior to a particular incident or event), B is the incident or particular *behaviour* causing concern itself, and C stands for *consequences* or effects of that behaviour. Such a framework lends itself to recording in 'performance' terms accurately (by direct observation) over any period of time. The references at the end of this section provide examples of A-B-C type recording charts.

The choice of any form of assessment observation schedule over another will largely depend on what precisely the teacher wishes to find out. If the child is already well known to the teacher, it is probably that both s/he and the child will have influenced each of their perceptions of the other; perhaps even distorted them. Research has demonstrated that teachers' observations of pupils with behaviour problems are often inaccurate as to the frequency and intensity of troublesome behaviour; teachers' observations can frequently become exaggerated or distorted.

To put a child's behaviour into perspective the teacher is advised to do some 'time sampling' - observation with a running diary-commentary, counting the number of times the undesired or troubling behaviour

14

occurs during the lesson or a portion of it and noting the setting of the classroom, rather than relying solely on the static framework of a check list.

A further disadvantage of most set formats (such as check lists) for recording behaviour is that they tend to pose negatively focused questions about the child, so that the whole ethos of the assessment becomes totally problem centred, and there seems very little that is positive to record about the child!

Recognising children in distress

Issues to do with bullying and child abuse including child sexual abuse (see references and Section 8) have been extensively researched in recent years. Although these phenomena have to be tackled at school and local levels (see Section 7), there is an onus on all teachers to be alert, as early as possible, to presenting signs, no matter how covertly they present. A considerable literature now exists, reference to some of which is included at the end of this section and in Section 8 which offers guidelines to teachers in recognising children experiencing bullying and/or abuse of any kind.

To summarize:

- identification and recognition should help the teacher to gather objective data;
- should help him/her to record current behaviour, including the type, frequency and severity;
- should help to record antecedent events or settings conditional to the behaviour;
- should help to build up a pattern of events and behaviour (remembering 'good' as well as 'bad');
- should help to sensitise teachers to recognising the child in distress, for example, as a consequence of bullying, abuse, family disruption;
- should assist the teacher to appraise her/his own attitude and classroom behaviour which may be negatively influencing children's behaviour;
- should help to set a cut-off point beyond which further personal intervention by the teacher is too difficult without help.

Postscript

The appendices contains two Observation Profiles. The idea behind this approach, described in the explanatory notes in the appendix, is that positive, as well as, negative behaviour needs to be identified and notes/records made of the situations and circumstances which elicit the behaviour. The teacher completing the Profile on a pupil is enabled to describe broader factors and influences on the behaviour in a variety of situations. An all-round picture can, thus, be constructed. The idea has been tried out effectively in schools.

Both these Observation Profiles are suitable for pupils evincing 'acting-out' behaviour, as well as those who show signs of distress.

Further reading

These references combine theory with practical approaches, and provide examples of observation, assessment and recording formats:

Bellack, A S and Hersen, M (1988) *Behavioural Assessment: A Practical Handbook,* Pergamon: Oxford.

Cheeseman, P L and Watts, P E (1985) *Positive Behaviour Management,* Croom Helm: London.

David, T (1993) *Child Protection and Early Years Teachers,* Open University Press: Buckingham.

Gillham, B (1991) *The Facts about Child Sexual Abuse,* Cassell: London.

Lennox, D (1991) *See Me After School,* David Fulton Publishers: London.

Rutter, M and Rutter, M (1992) *Developing Minds, Challenge and Continuity Across the Life Span,* Penguin Books: Harmondsworth.

Tattum, D and Lane, D (Eds) (1980) *Bullying in Schools,* Trentham Books: Stoke-on-Trent.

Tattum, D and Herbert, G (1993) *Countering Bullying,* Trentham Books: Stoke-on-Trent.

Wheldall, K, Merrett, F and Glynn, T (1986) *Behaviour Analysis in Educational Psychology,* Croom Helm: London.

Wielkiewicz, R M (1986) *Behaviour Management in Schools,* Trentham Books: Stoke-on-Trent.

Section 3 - Some Effective Teaching Strategies

Some teachers appear to have less difficulty than others in creating effective learning environments for their pupils. A well-run classroom, with a low potential for inappropriate behaviour can, of itself, have beneficial effects in both learning and adjustment of so-called 'difficult' pupils.

What are the main issues to be considered?

Teacher behaviour

It is through the teacher's behaviour that control is established, usually through non-verbal communication. Each of the following is associated with effective classroom control:

- appropriate eye and physical contact with pupils;
- relaxed body movements;
- relaxed, controlled verbal behaviour;
- ability to achieve silence quickly with a class group;
- ability to move physically through the territory of all the students in the classroom;
- keeping all reprimands brief;
- giving clear directives with no back-tracking;
- body language and verbal utterances in synchrony;
- resisting student/pupil-instigated interruptions.

Teacher planning: the classroom environment

The physical environment of the classroom affects pupils' responses. Paying attention to the following can maintain positive pupil behaviour:

- noise level - different activities should be conducted at different levels of acceptable classroom noise;
- design of buildings/classrooms - some activities may be very difficult to carry out because of the basic design or size of the classroom;
- acknowledgement of individual pupil's need for space - pupils need privacy within the classroom;
- different activities need different seating arrangements - the teacher needs to arrange the location of materials, patterns of pupil movement and seating arrangements;
- in each activity or lesson, the teacher must decide whether s/he goes to pupils or they go to him/her; this reinforces the notion of what kinds of pupil-behaviour are expected in each type of activity.

Enhancing learning in activities/lessons

How activities or lessons are carried out by a teacher will substantially affect pupil participation and response. The following pointers are associated with effective lesson/activity progress:

- ensure that the activity begins on time with all pupils already engaged;
- ensure that the objectives of the activity are clear to all pupils in advance;
- ensure that different pupils' abilities and skills are acknowledged beforehand;
- ensure that pupils are aware of personal and group targets by the end of the activity or lesson time;
- ensure that all work is finished when and where it needs to be;
- ensure even attention is spread around the room;
- in open activities, ensure that attention does not become focussed on one individual or small group;
- praise effort continually by giving comments and feedback on pupil performance;
- ask open questions to facilitate dialogue and encourage the pupil to offer comment, explanation, description;
- allow pupils to ask for help;
- keep all pupils busy making them account for the time they spend.

Activity/lesson planning

Most teachers have experience of an activity or lesson 'dying on its feet'. At such times the teacher knows only too well the effect that this has on the behaviour of pupils. The importance of planning lessons carefully is taken as read, but other related aspects are worth bearing in mind.

- if possible, minimize all interruptions, intrusions from outside the classroom, i.e. 'phone calls, notes from the secretary, notes brought into the room by other pupils;
- ensure that all materials are available before the activity begins;
- set clear boundaries between one activity or lesson and another. If possible, bring pupils together as a group at the beginning and end of activities;
- intervene quietly if possible at the earliest opportunity if an individual or group is beginning to exhibit inappropriate behaviour, i.e. do not let a situation build up;
- do not confront pupils in public if the issue can be better dealt with in private.

The following texts are recommended to readers wishing to follow up the headings:

Further reading

Bull, S and Solity, J (1987) *Classroom Management: Principles to Practice,* Croom Helm: London.

Cheeseman, P L and Watts, P E (1985) *Positive Behaviour Management: A Manual for Teachers,* Croom Helm: London.

Cohen, L and Cohen, A (Eds) (1987) *Disruptive Behaviour: A Source Book for Teachers,* Harper and Row: London.

Lovitt, T C (1984) *Tactics for Teaching,* Charles E. Merrill: Columbus.

Robertson, J (1989) *Effective Classroom Control* (2nd Edition), Hodder and Stoughton: London.

Tattum, D (Ed) (1986) *Management of Disruptive Pupil Behaviour in Schools,* John Wiley: Chichester.

Thomas, G (1992) 'Ecological Interventions', in Wolfendale, S, Bryans, T, Fox M, Labram, A, Sigston, A (Eds) *The Profession and Practice of Educational Psychology, Future Directions,* Cassell: London.

Section 4 - Individual Programmes and Group Work

In the last section, consideration was given to the general environment of the classroom and to how the behaviour of the teacher relates to whole groups of pupils. Implementing the suggestions and pedagogic practices set out in Section 3 will almost certainly reduce the frequency of inappropriate behaviour and maintain a brisker pace of learning for most pupils.

However, even if such a near-ideal situation is achieved, there will still be a number of children who give cause for concern and who may need more specifically-focussed, individually based programmes of behaviour and learning management before real progress can be achieved.

Before such intervention is started, there are two good practical rules to consider, then follow:

- First, begin with low-key interventions which can be incorporated into the normal pattern of the teaching day. For example, singling the child for special praise and attention when effort and settled behaviour are in evidence; clarifying to the child exactly what s/he has to do; ignoring minor misdemeanours or attention-seeking behaviours.

- Secondly, give all attempts to intervene time to take effect. There is a lot of evidence to suggest that once the teacher becomes aware of a pupil's problem(s), s/he is increasingly preoccupied with them, and becomes discouraged because, for a time, the teacher's words or actions and the increased observations of the pupil's misdemeanours overlap.

There are other factors to bear in mind when trying to set up an individual learning and/or behaviour programme.

- Just as identified problems are construed within age appropriate or social contexts, setting up an intervention programme may also have to take these contexts into account. (This may limit the possibilities.)
- Try to get help and support from another teacher in the school, a support teacher, head of year or educational psychologist during observation sessions. You do not need to take on the child's difficulties as a challenge to your own self-esteem or professional competence!
- Children's home circumstances and their reaction to them vary greatly; some pupils are resilient in the most dire surroundings, others react to relatively mild disturbances. In the role of teacher or welfare

assistant there may be very little which can be done directly to enhance the child's home environment, so try to focus on within-school factors which are amenable to change - and change by you.

- Behavioural change in pupils occurs with changes in consequences and changes in teachers' behaviour which, often inadvertently, can reinforce bad behaviour as well as reduce it.

Most problems that appear in school and which cause concern are those which threaten the stability and harmonious functioning of a class or group. Consequently, withdrawn or unforthcoming children may receive little teacher support or extra attention. Others may come to the notice of the staff because they commit anti-social acts during unsupervised periods of the school day or out of school hours.

Steps in setting up a programme

The most effective individualised programmes must begin with observation of what the pupil is actually doing and not, as so often happens, with what the pupil is already labelled as being (e.g. 'disruptive', 'inattentive' or 'lazy'). This must also include recording positive and acceptable behaviour.

Observation

Section 2 refers to some of the scales, check lists and observation techniques currently in use. The selection of one particular method or scale will be a matter of professional judgement in terms of the age of the pupils, ease of use and relevance (also see Section 8 and Appendix).

Formulating teaching aims: using a behavioural approach as an example

Having established the occurrence, frequency and intensity of the difficult behaviour (but again bearing in mind the value of low-key intervention at first and the minimal disruption to teaching patterns rule mentioned earlier) it is then appropriate to attempt setting up easily-attainable, broad teaching aims for the pupil, based firmly on the observations of what the problems really are, *so that a way can be devised to ensure success for the child.*

Thus, for example:

Problem	*Aim for teaching*
Duane finds arithmetic difficult.	Duane will count accurately to 100 by the end of the term.
Sally is withdrawn in class.	Sally will play a co-operative sharing game with another pupil once a day until Easter.

21

Maintaining a series of these kinds of realistic and attainable teaching aims for an individual pupil over a period of weeks or months may often result in increased motivation on the part of the child and more settled integrated behaviour in class.

Setting up objectives

Having attempted to intervene with a pupil's learning or behaviour difficulty by low key actions in terms of maintaining broad teaching aims, and having allowed enough time for them to take effect, it may be that a more carefully detailed formulation of precise objectives is necessary for some children if further progress is to be achieved.

The reference to behavioural objectives is justified at this point because there is often confusion between, and among, teachers about exactly what the pupil should be trying to do. (There is usually less doubt what s/he is actually doing wrong!) A behavioural objective is a specific goal which outlines:

a. the behaviour required *(e.g. Winnie will point)*;
b. the situation or context *(when given three different coloured blocks)*;
c. criteria for deciding whether or not the goal has been achieved *(to give the blue block on request five out of five times)*.

For an older child an example goal could be:

a. *John will hand in neat copies of his homework;*
b. *in each subject set;*
c. *daily, for two weeks.*

Verbal or written contracts

Contracts are a way of formalizing interchanges between individuals - teachers and pupils, parents and children. They have the advantage of focussing all parties to the contract on the future, rather than trawling over the traumas of the past. They are also useful in that parents, pupils, teachers and classroom assistants can act reasonably on the other to maintain the contract. Contracts also establish a forum for dialogue and compromise in such a way that successful negotiation will involve positive reinforcement. A good model of behaviour is thereby established.

A written contract spells out precisely the responsibilities and actions of each of the parties, and sets out who will do what, when and how often. It provides an agreed framework for all concerned. Sample written contracts are given in Cheeseman and Watts (1985) p.149.

Social skills teaching

Social skills teaching may be seen as a positive way of using school time with social, behaviour or emotional problems to learn new skills which will enable them to behave in different, more effective and more congenial ways. Social skills may be an essential part of the curriculum for some children, emphasizing particular kinds of social 'survival' skills, some of which are crucial not only to relationships but equally to 'academic' achievement. It is not possible here to provide an inventory of all the possible social skills which are amenable to school work, but some headings could be:

classroom skills	- putting away books; - noting homework; - always carrying equipment.
interaction skills	- not interrupting; - listening attentively; - making eye contact; - taking turns.
personal skills	- washing their own clothes; - keeping clean; - brushing teeth.

Individual children need different emphases. Withdrawn pupils particularly benefit from the precise behavioural, step-by-step nature of social skills teaching, so that areas of personal difficulty can be shared and worked on with support from other pupils.

Summarised advice

1. Begin by observing what the pupil does, as a result of what, and with what consequences.
2. Observe how often and when it happens.
3. Set up low key positive interventions first of all.
4. Give time for these to work.
5. Always monitor your own behaviour in terms of accidental reward of the pupil's inappropriate behaviour.

Further reading

Cartledge, G and Milburn, J F (1986) *Teaching Social Skills to Children*, Pergamon: New York.

Cheeseman, P L and Watts, P E (1985) *Positive Behaviour Management: A Manual for Teachers*, Croom Helm: London.

Coulby, D and Harper, T (1985) *Preventing Classroom Disruption: Policy Practice and Evaluation in Urban Schools*, Croom Helm: London.

Essa, E (1990) *A Practical Guide to Solving Pre-school Behaviour Problems* (2nd Edition), Delmar Publications: New York.

Hughes, J (1988) *Cognitive Behaviour Therapy with Children in Schools*, Pergamon: New York.

Lovitt, T C (1984) *Tactics for Teaching*, Charles E. Merrill: Columbus.

Raymond, J (1985) *Implementing Pastoral Care in Schools*, Croom Helm: London.

Scherer, M, Gersch, I and Fry, L (Eds) (1990) *Meeting Disruptive Behaviour*, Macmillan: Basingstoke.

Section 5 - Involving Pupils in Learning and Behaviour Management

Review of developments and ideas

The direct inclusion of children themselves in planning, managing and reviewing their own learning progress is very recent. For so long, pupils of all ages have been seen as the unquestioning recipients of prior-planned lessons and homework assignment. The only points of direct consultation with them have been, at secondary level, at subject choice and option times. After years of having little or no choice, pupils are quite suddenly confronted with important questions of choice.

Latterly though, and belatedly, the pupils' perspective is being increasingly considered to be a valid part of collective educational decision-making, particularly as evidence mounts that there is a clear, positive association between pupil input into a variety of specified activities and enhanced motivation and feelings of self-worth on their part. The *Code of Practice* (1994) builds participation at each of the five stages. Children from infant to secondary phases are encouraged to:

- set and organise learning goals;
- monitor their own progress;
- estimate their learning, personal and social assets and problems;
- describe their preferred tasks and subject areas;
- work co-operatively with peers.

It is compatible with a movement over time to regard education in broader terms than just passing on subject-based knowledge and skills, to perceive that the young learner could have more to offer the educational process than simply being taught.

Examples from four main areas of pupils' involvement are given below. They include instances from infant, junior and secondary age-phases.

1 - Self-assessment of development and progress in school

There is first-hand evidence that children as young as three can comment upon their acquisition of skills and growing independence, and can have views upon family relationships and their own behaviour. In a pilot study into the feasibility of a parent-completed early years profile, the involvement of young children themselves was encouraged. Whilst their parents acted as mediators, the mode of response on a significant number of the completed *All About Me* booklets, indicated the direct participation of a number of children aged from three to six (Wolfendale 1990). From the type of responses they recorded (in reality, by their mothers on their behalf) these children held definite views and had articulate feelings on a variety of aspects of their lives.

At primary school stage there is an example of effective self-reporting and self-appraisal of progress in school using the *This is Me* assessment form, which covers the areas: at home; my school; I am good at; when I grow up; things I find hard; my friends (Mitchell 1993).

Within secondary school milieux, the most researched and best developed area is that of pupil profiling, particularly connected with *Records of Achievement*. Typically, secondary age students comment upon their work likes, dislikes, strengths and weaknesses; record their in and out of school interests; express their views about their personal qualities, career and future aspirations, hopes and fears in general.

The idea is being taken on board within the special needs context, too. One example is that of the *child report*, the child's contribution to formal assessment. A self-report written by Peter, a 13-year-old referred for 'emotional and behavioural disorder' (EBD), which was his contribution to a 1981 Act assessment is reproduced in *Figure 1 on Page 28* (and see Gersch 1992).

2 - Self-reporting and recording

This area is, of course, related to the previous one (above), but refers more to self-monitoring and self-reporting of progress through a behaviour change or learning management programme (see Section 4). Most of the evidence shows a clear change in positive directions: towards acceptable behaviour or increased time spent 'on task', especially when pupils are thus directly involved in devising the programme. A number of American studies indicated that self-monitoring clearly has potential to become a standard technique for use with children. As both an assessment and intervention procedure, it offers a practical and efficient means to collect data and evaluate the progress of intervention procedures. 'Home grown' approaches include the *Steps to Success* technique developed by Thacker (see references).

3 - Co-operative learning and peer tutoring

Peer tutoring has recently received considerable attention since studies, mainly in the area of reading, reveal gains made by the 'tutee' and, in some instances, when the peer tutor may also have specified learning needs, s/he can also benefit in measurable as well as qualitative ways. Same-age or cross-age peer tutoring is characterised by these features: pupil pairs, one of whom acts as the 'tutor'; a 'play teacher' game in which one of the pair takes on the teacher role; shared, paired learning in duo.

Group work in classrooms has been a focus of attention for a number of years, but recently there has been particular notice paid to the benefits of co-operative learning, as opposed to the static nature of merely easing physical proximity. Co-operative learning, at primary and secondary levels, can be defined as group work with any one or more of these aims: collaboration on a specific project, i.e. shared learning; mutual co-operation and assistance; learning to work in parallel as well as solo; incorporating social interaction with attention to the task in hand. Projects have taken place in infant and junior school and also in a secondary school where pupils' and teachers' attitudes to co-operative work were explored. These studies indicated that there have been a number of issues that need resolution as a prerequisite for the incorporation of group work routinely into the school, such as sympathy for and acceptance of the ideas by other staff members, if not their active involvement.

The considerable amount of experimental American work in this area suggests that peer-influenced interventions can be effective and can offer increased teaching and learning opportunities.

4 - Personal and social education
Many teachers and educational psychologists have carried out short social learning and pastorally focussed programmes in schools, which are characterised by:

• explicit rule setting from the outset, e.g. turn-taking, not interrupting;
• agreed rewards and sanctions, e.g. stars, tokens;
• focus on empathy and prosocial skills;
• pre-and post-baseline measurement.

A personal/social skill programme at a residential special school for boys with behavioural and emotional difficulties has also been described (McConnon 1988). In this and other examples, we see the powerful effects of peer interaction and peer influence working positively upon attitudes and behaviour, providing there is a constructive and supportive setting provided by the teachers and other staff.

These four areas of pupil involvement are characterized by a number of features in common. These include:

a. explicit prior consultation with, and between, the pupils themselves;
b. direct negotiation with them;
c. an agreement, even in some cases a contractual agreement, to participate;
d. an enjoyment (social) element to parallel the instructional component;
e. a finite aspect to each initiative so that pupils have an overview of the exercise and retain some control of it.

A discussion on pupil involvement cannot conclude without reference to the legitimacy of their broader participation within the life of the school. It would be consistent with the principles and practices advocated in Section 7 for pupils to be consulted, and to have their views on maintaining effective and just discipline, sanctions and pastoral systems. It could be argued that they have rights to be involved in planning and maintaining such systems; study of the psychology of motivation indicates increased commitment when an issue is shared and corporately 'owned'. Confrontation and alienation are likely to be reduced if pupils, teachers and parents know that consultative forums exist for the purposes of problem sharing and solving.

Sometimes when I misbehave it's because I'm thinking about how my brother behaves but I don't want to end up like him.

I want to go to a school where they will make me behave properly even if it means locking me in a room by myself with no windows and one light and a desk where I have to do my work.

I like maths and English. I would like to go to a school in the country because I like nature studies. I would like to go to a boarding school because at the moment I never do what my mum and dad tell me to and this makes them and me unhappy.

Signed ___Peter___

Figure 1 - Peter's contribution to his own assessment/statement:

Further reading

Cowie, H (1987) 'Co-operative groupwork in the secondary school: teachers' and pupils' perspectives', *Educational and Child Psychology*, Vol 4, 3 and 4, pp 19-29.

Gersch, I 'Pupil involvement in assessment' in Cline, T (Ed) (1992) *The Assessment of SEN International Perspectives*, Routledge: London.

Mahler, C A and Zins, J E (Eds) (1987) *Psycho-educational Intervention in the Schools*, Pergamon: Oxford.

McConnon, S (1988) 'A programme for pupils' choices', *British Journal of Special Education*, 15, 4, pp. 147-149.

Mitchell, S (1993) *'This is Me'* Profile. Contact author at Camden EPS, Richard Cobden School, Camden Street, London NW1 0LL.

Mortimore, P, Sammons, P, Stoll, L, and Ecob, R (1988) *School Matters - the Junior Years*, Open Books: Wells.

Raymond, J (1985) *Implementing Pastoral Care in Schools*, Croom Helm: London.

Reason, R, Rooney, S and Joffe, M (1987) 'Co-operative learning in an infants' school' *Education and Child Psychology*, 4, 3 and 4, pp 40-49.

Thacker, J *Steps to Success: An Interpersonal Problem-solving Approach for Children*, NFER-Nelson: Windsor.

Topping, K (1987) *The Peer Tutoring Handbook: Promoting Co-operative Learning*, Croom Helm: London.

Wolfendale, S (1992) *Primary Schools and Special Needs: Policy, Planning and Provision (2nd edition)*, Cassell: London.

Wolfendale, S (1990) *'All About Me'* booklet published by NES-Arnold, Ludlow Hill Road, West Bridgford, Nottingham NG2 6HD.

Section 6 - Working Co-operatively with Parents

Whereas direct consultation with pupils over their own learning is still fairly novel (see Section 5), consultation with parents has become, if not a standard feature in all schools, nevertheless an integral part of the work at many nursery, primary and secondary schools. The parental presence is visible and vocal not just in association with discreet, finite projects, but routinely in a variety of ways summarized below.

Recent educational legislation (*Educational Reform Act 1988, Education (Schools) Act 1992, Education Act 1993*) has put a high premium on parental choice and has created structures for the expression of parental views on a variety of educational issues. Hand in hand with such formal structures, there are now many examples of effective parent-teacher co-operation which have created a momentum for home-school links that will ensure productive partnership in the years to come (Wolfendale, 1992). The Code of Practice (1994) brings together the legislative context and recent initiatives to clarify the respective responsibilities of schools, teachers, parents, LEA personnel, in meeting special educational needs. One of the key principles of the Code of Practice, reiterated throughout, is the necessity of all concerned to work in partnership.

The relationship is reinforced by the inclusion into schools' inspection format (under the *Education (Schools) Act 1992*) of the requirement for inspection teams to hold a parents' meeting and to record parents' views about the school.

Areas of co-operation

The table below summarizes the major initiatives of the last few years. References are provided in the 'Further reading' section for these areas of innovation.

Major areas of parental involvement at home

Parents in school
- helping with reading, mathematics, other curriculum areas.

Parents as educators at home
- home-based programmes: in reading, language development, maths;
- Portage schemes.

Home-school links
- written communication (e.g. newsletters);
- home-school council, parent-tutor groups, curriculum plans to parents;

- school brochures for parents, reporting to parents under the *Education (Schools) Act 1992.*

Community education/community
- parents' room in schools;
- parents and others attending classes in school;
- local and national parents' associations, parents' support groups;
- LEA community education.

Parents as governors
- parent governors, parents on nursery and play group management;

Parents and special needs
- parental involvement in referral, in formal assessment and reviews;
- involvement in behaviour and learning programmes.

From this work, a number of findings emerge of relevance to this section:

- that parents' supreme position as 'primary educators' of their children can be utilized to assist them to learn;
- that the skills involved in parenting can complement teachers' skills on behalf of children;
- that the milieu of home can be as conducive a setting for enhancing childrens' learning at school, for different but equally valid reasons.

A resumé of possible ways of involving parents in behaviour and learning management in three areas will demonstrate current work and point the way to their extension into more schools. Specific references to initiatives appear in the 'Further Reading' list.

1. Involving parents in the assessment of development and progress

Evidence from the UK and America suggests that parents' accuracy of judgement on their own children is to be trusted; that is, they show skills of relatively impartial observation and assessment of performance and behaviour, and often these judgements do accord with those of professionals. Parents' descriptions of completion of profiles provide invaluable first-hand information about what the child is like at home, which may or may not concur with teachers' perspectives about progress and behaviour in school. This parental dimension can also provide a baseline or starting point on which to plan behaviour change programmes.

Considerable work has been done at pre-school level. (See the *Portage Check List* and also Section 5 for a reference to *All About Me.*)

The concept of the *parental profile,* or description of the child at home, has been extensively researched in real-life settings. This idea involves parents in the use of guidelines piloted, revised and made available to mothers and fathers of children from pre-school through to secondary age, as an aid to constructing a parental profile. The approach can be used for parents' routine assessment of progress as well as for their contribution to assessments. At the end of this section, the profile on Peter (see Section 5), written by his parents as their contribution for a formal assessment, is reproduced. (See also Wolfendale (1992, 1993) for a proposed Model of Reciprocal Reporting).

2. Working with parents on behaviour-change programmes
2.1. Observations and recording
The idea of teacher and/or parent-completed charts is no longer new. It was originally propagated within behavioural contexts as a means of observing, then recording, antecedent behaviour via a tally or other means of counting to build up an accurate picture of setting, or causing, events, their frequency and type as a starting point for behavioural-change programmes.

Such approaches, even in diluted form, are found to be useful ways of pinpointing behaviour which causes concern at school or home. Some obvious examples are:

- aggressive behaviour;
- distractible behaviour;
- unco-operative behaviour;
- task avoidance;
- annoying habits (e.g. pencil tapping, nail-biting, chair pushing).

It might be thought that the complexities of social interaction, including non-verbal behaviour, cannot be captured in a simple recording instrument. In fact, it can provide a way in to problem identification, a vehicle for the various participants to explore and clarify troubling behaviour. As a device it also facilitates the prioritization of problems to be tackled for, as behaviours are highlighted, recorded and then discussed, the relative severity and tractability of them become apparent. This systematic approach of dealing with one difficulty at a time may also reduce other behaviour that is reported by teachers and parents to be upsetting and disruptive.

2.2. Individual programmes
More practical work is carried out in this way by teachers and parents, very often supported by educational psychologists and support teachers than is reported publicly, because it is core practice work to those

concerned. During the last few years, we have become familiar with target and goal setting, and devising learning and behaviour programmes which are based on task analysis and which are sequential.

That parents can act as key agents and 'teachers' in these initiatives is amply demonstrated by Portage schemes, which also empirically nails the myth that the most effective and willing parents acting as educators can only be articulate and well-educated themselves.

Section 4, as well as the 'Further reading' list in this section gives reference to books and manuals which can help those wishing to set up programmes to help children learn effectively and relevantly, or to work with parents as well as with pupils to reduce disruptive, anxiety-provoking behaviour and promote desirable conduct.

2.3. Working with groups of parents
Some workers and researchers have advocated, and some have tried for themselves, effecting changes by working with groups of parents for these reasons:

(a) to provide a forum for collective support and to share problems, stress and difficulties;
(b) to create a setting in which solutions to problems and ideas for action can be generated more effectively within a group than in a one-to one interview or counselling session;
(c) to enhance parental confidence and skills in dealing with behaviour problems at home and through group encouragement.

Group work can take place within the school, in a schools' psychological service or child guidance context, or at a neutral venue such as a community meeting place. Reported advantages of this approach include not only improvements in behaviour by some children, but also a reduction in anxiety in some parents. An increase in group cohesiveness when the parents in the group come from the same school (so to speak) can also be a welcome spin-off that benefits the home-school community (see reference to *Anti-Bullying Materials* in Section 8).

3. A whole-school approach for involving parents in behaviour and learning management
One reference (Wolfendale 1990) offers practical steps that can be taken to incorporate parental perspectives and input into the whole-school approach discussed in Section 7. It would be consistent of shared, and a sharing of, responsibility for discipline and sanction systems as well as for positive programmes designed to bring about behaviour change, to consult with parents as well as with pupils.

Our major concern at this time is to find Peter a school which we can be sure he will attend. We are very concerned about the amount of time he has missed already.

We have tried taking him to school and returning him to school when he has run away but we still cannot prevent him from not attending.

At home, Peter refuses to accept our rules. If he cannot have his own way he starts to lose his temper and throw things around. His behaviour at the moment is out of hand. He does not respond to any punishment we try to impose.

We are also very worried at the moment because Peter cannot settle at night and we are worried that he will wander away. We would like his tendency to run away from difficult situations to be taken into account when his new school is being chosen.

We feel that we cannot guarantee his attendance at any day school as he is very determined when he does not wish to be there. For these reasons, we are asking you to find Peter a boarding school place.

Signed: Peter's parents

Figure 2 - The parental contribution for a formal assessment for Peter.

Further reading

Atkin, J Bastiani, J and Goode, J (1988) *Listening to Parents*, Croom Helm: London.

Hinton, S (1993) *The ABC of Behaviour: Troubleshooting for Parents of Very Young Children.* Available from: Surrey LEA, Room 189B, County Hall, Kingston-upon-Thames, KT1 2DJ.

Hornby, G (1987) *Parent to Parent Scheme* - contact at Hull University, School of Education, 173 Cottingham Road, Hull, HU5 2EH.

McConkey, R (1985) *Working with Parents: A Practical Guide for Teachers and Therapists*, Croom Helm: London.

Topping, K (1986) *Parents as Educators*, Croom Helm: London.

Wolfendale, S (1990) 'Involving parents in behaviour management: a whole-school approach' in Scherer, M, Gersch, I, Fry, L (eds) *Meeting Disruptive Behaviour*, Macmillan: Basingstoke.

Wolfendale, S (1988) *The Parental Contribution to Assessment,* NASEN Enterprises: Stafford. (Out of print)

Wolfendale, S (1992) *Empowering Parents and Teachers - Working with Children,* Cassell: London.

Wolfendale, S (ed) (1993) Chapter 9 in *Assessing Special Educational Needs,* Cassell: London.

Section 7 - Whole-school Policies: Realities and Imperatives

Since the first edition of this booklet was published in 1989, the educational landscape has changed substantially. Aspects of school life were hitherto not open to outside scrutiny, nor accountable beyond the confines of the school or a select number of LEA personnel. Schools no longer have the option as to whether or not they choose to adopt policies, e.g. on special educational needs, parents, discipline.

In the climate of the 1990's, it is now imperative, indeed driven by legislation, for schools to have declared written accountable policies on many aspects of schooling. The 'secret garden' has been opened up.

As far as school policy on discipline and behaviour management is concerned, the key forces for change have been:

- the *Elton Report* (1989) which gives clear recommendations for whole-school policy on discipline;
- the *Education (Schools) Act, 1992* which mandates compulsory periodic independent inspection of schools, via OFSTED, and which sets out detailed performance criteria by which pupil behaviour and discipline in schools will be judged, including attendance rates;
- the *Education Act, 1993* (based on the government White Paper of 1992, *Choice and Diversity* which deals with 'children who behave badly, (para. 1.54) including children who truant or are excluded.)
- the *Education Act, 1993* Part 3 (para. 161) which requires all schools and governing bodies to have SEN policies;
- the Code of Practice (1994), which spells out the nature and content of schools' SEN policies, a key requirement of which is that *every* school should have a designated SEN co-ordinator.

During the 1980's, accumulated research clearly indicated that some primary and secondary schools were more successful than others in producing a cohesive education for the majority of their pupils. The characteristics which define the effective school (Fullan, 1992; Reynolds and Cuttance, 1992) are now beyond dispute. Schools are now, therefore, equipped with the knowledge and an understanding of the relevant processes, to become effective learning institutions.

This has been acknowledged in the Code of Practice (1994). For the first time, publicly, schools have been delegated explicit responsibilities in the earlier Stages (i.e. Stages 1 and 2) without external support from the LEA, to identify, monitor and provide for the special educational needs of their pupils. This will involve the forging of new partnerships and networks of communication both within schools, their teaching staff, and their governing bodies as well as co-ordination between schools and LEAs.

A number of other points can be made from the available research on school organization and learning/behaviour problems. These parallel the theme in Section 3 on effective teaching where the evidence was cited that particular kinds of classrooms and teacher behaviours reduce (or increase) the incidence of individually appearing problems.

Cooper (1993) suggests that, 'the first step along the road to increased effectiveness is an exercise in self-analysis' (p248). He poses 17 key questions that schools need to ask themselves, many of which have been addressed in this booklet.

There are a number of within-school issues which need to be addressed:

- Most disruptive behaviour or poor achievement by unacceptably large numbers of pupils can only be reduced by prevention organised through coherent school policies.
- Special remedial or behavioural groups do not, on the whole, have much effect because they simply 'displace' rather than deal with the perceived problem.
- Teachers with special responsibilities for integration, support or welfare of particular pupils are unlikely to have very much effect on the overall ethos of a school if their work remains confined only to these selected pupils.
- If a school, in order to maintain discipline, commits itself to a set of sanctions or punishments, these will quickly become divisive. Lower-achieving children fall foul of these much more frequently and become more anti-authority in the later years of schooling than do better achievers, thus defeating the purpose of the rules and sanctions.
- Whatever a pupil's social or home background, the educational environment of the school exerts a powerful influence on the child's self-esteem and feeling of self-worth, or lack of it.
- Many self-evident problems of behaviour and learning arise from communication difficulties between and among teaching staff, and the denial or misrepresentation of previous events within the school before a particular crisis occurs.
- Many teachers believe their pupils' problems are caused by the children's home backgrounds. Most parents believe their children's difficulties are caused by the school. This mismatch or perception needs to be addressed as an integral part of a parental involvement policy.

The key characteristics associated with a positive educational experience for pupils are:

- a prompt start to lesson;
- high emphasis on academic achievement;
- low emphasis on punishment;
- high recognition of pupils' positive achievement;
- well-cared for buildings;
- evidence of pupils' work on display.

Implications for whole school policies

What are the implications of these summarized research findings for the creation of whole-school policies?

The Elton Report endorsed its own recommendation for all schools to have coherent policies on discipline and behaviour management by including extracts from a number of such policies already developed by schools (pp 283 - 292). Some of the major components include: rewards and sanctions; fostering pride in school, and ownership of discipline issues.

It is axiomatic that a whole school policy applies to all personnel who:

- play their part in its formulation;
- fully understand and agree with it;
- share responsibility for its successful implementation.

By all personnel, we mean of course:

- teaching staff;
- governors;
- non-teaching staff;
- pupils;
- parents.

Again, as Elton makes clear, a whole-school policy must go beyond a rule-rewards-sanctions view of school discipline to encompass issues of principle and equal opportunities. That is, there need to be statements of intent about:

- anti-racism and dealing with racial harassment;
- anti-sexism, and gender equality;
- anti-bullying measures;
- recognition of, and action in respect of, child abuse within the context of agreed local child protection procedures;
- monitoring attendance and acting swiftly upon lapses;
- exclusions (in line with 1993 Education Act).

The purpose of a whole-school policy on behaviour and discipline is to ensure:

- Firstly, that problems do not arise in the first place, or are minimised;
- Secondly, that, when they do occur, practice measures are in place to reduce their impact on the smooth running of the institution.

School inspection requirements *(Framework for Inspection 1993, 2nd edition)* include performance indicators such as: attendance, behaviour, and discipline, pupils' entitlement to 'proper' spiritual and moral development, as well as their personal and social needs. In keeping with these requirements, and in readiness for periodic inspection, schools will need to build in a policy monitoring and review cycle which, again, involves all personnel.

Other Policy Components to be considered
Rules and Sanctions

It is a relatively easy matter to draw up a list of school rules, but it is extremely difficult to enforce them in a way that does not unfairly discriminate against some pupils. Not only do different teachers interpret and apply them in different ways, but they rarely inform the teacher as to what s/he is expected to do when a rule is being infringed. Variability of teachers' responses leads, in time, to 'staff inconsistencies' which is one decisive factor in producing anti-social attitudes and disaffection among pupils.

All personnel, in a suitable joint forum, need to ask questions along the lines of:

- Who is the rule for?
- Who decided on the rule?
- How is it to be enforced?
- What do the staff actually do to enforce it?
- Will the rule create increased staff-pupil confrontation?
- Are there better alternatives to that rule?
- Will all the rules be underpinned by an agreed code of practice to which all pupils, staff and parents contribute?

Staff consistency

School staff are not a homogeneous group of professionals who view school organisation or processes in a similar way. Consequently, there are considerable management variations of children by individual staff - not just to do with school rules, but with many other interchanges throughout the school day. These inconsistencies often lie at the root of many reported incidents of disruption, i.e. the pupil did not know what to expect from a particular teacher, so did not realize his/her behaviour was inappropriate until reprimanded.

The more inconsistency in teacher-pupil exchanges there are, the more likely it is that there will be a corresponding increase in the number of reported incidents of disruption or unsettled behaviour. Staff consistency is essential in a number of other crucial areas of teacher-pupil contact. These include:

- entering or leaving classes;
- praising pupils' efforts;
- supervising pupils in and out of lessons;
- setting homework assignments and marking them promptly;
- agreement on appropriate courses of action when a crisis occurs.

Staff support
Some schools have a system which offers staff support, especially necessary for example when a teacher faces a difficulty in the teaching of a particular pupil or group. This often means a reappraisal of the whole structure of internal communication within the school and/or a year group, so that advice and support is directed to the teacher in such a way that his/her self esteem and competence are not undermined, but enhanced. Likewise, non-teaching staff are equally entitled to the backing of senior teaching staff in matters of discipline.

Supportive education
For many pupils disaffection and poor progress in school are related directly to inappropriate curricula. Recent DFE funded research (O'Keeffe and Stoll at the University of North London, not yet published) suggests, furthermore, that a significant number of secondary pupils elect to truant from specific lessons and curriculum areas, as they perceive these to be boring and irrelevant.

Further reading
Bell, P and Best, R (1986) *Supportive Education, An Integrated Response to Pastoral Care and Special Needs,* Simon and Schuster: London.

Cooper, P (1993) *Effective Schools for Disaffected Students,* Routledge: London.

Elton, Lord R C (Chair) (1989) *Discipline in Schools,* HMSO: London.

Fullan, M (1992) *Successful School Improvement,* Open University Press: Buckingham.

Galloway, D and Goodwin, C (1987) *The Education of Disturbing Children,* Longman: London.

Mortimore, P, Sammons, P, Stoll, L, Lewis, D, and Ecob, R (1988) *School Matters - the Junior Years,* Open Books: London.

NASEN (1993) *Special Educational Needs and Legislation: A Guide to the Education Act 1993 and OFSTED Inspections,* NASEN Enterprises: Stafford.

OFSTED (1993) *Framework For Inspection* (2nd Edition), HMSO: London.

O'Keefe, D and Stoll, P (in press) *Truancy in English Secondary Schools,* HMSO:London.

Reynolds, D and Cuttance, P (Eds) (1992) *School Effectiveness, Research, Policy and Practice,* Cassell: London.

Tattum, D P (Ed) (1986) *Management of Disruptive Pupil Behaviour in Schools,* John Wiley: Chichester.

Watkins, C and Wagner, P (1987) *School Discipline: A Whole-School Approach,* Basil Blackwell: London.

Wolfendale, S (1992) *Primary Schools and Special Needs: Policy, Planning and Provision* (2nd Edition), Cassell: London.

Section 8 - A Treasury of Resources to Support a Policy of Behaviour Management and Inservice Training

A: A selected, annotated review of resources
B: Bullying: resources, training, advice packs, videos, organisations

This final section addresses inservice training and support; offers basic guiding principles, and describes INSET packs currently available in the area of behaviour management. This includes bullying, as this has, rightly, become an area of major concern.

Inservice training principles and practice

There was expansion of INSET in this area as a result of the recommendations from the Elton Committee. Whichever INSET models are utilized, and whichever packs are considered to be most applicable for particular purposes, one major guiding principle needs to be borne in mind, namely that, irrespective of the frequency or degree of severity of troublesome or troubling behaviour, other contextual factors must be taken into account.

We have sought in this handbook to present the major influences impinging upon 'offending' and 'worrying' behaviour and to demonstrate that teachers, albeit often inadvertently, may aggravate or predispose problems to develop. Now, we reiterate the point made at the outset: that society should not expect teachers to have to cope with behaviour that has gone beyond the containable within ordinary schools, whatever the reasons or precipitating causes.

The moral imperative that underlies all interventions with pupil behaviour is that teachers should satisfy themselves that all analyses and school-based strategies have reasonably been tried within the context of whole-school policy; and schools in general ought to seek external help for behaviour resistant to internal methods only when the collective responsibility advocated in Section 7 has been seen to be in operation and has reached its limits. Severe individual behaviour disturbance and maladjustment remains a societal responsibility, along a spectrum of behaviour that embraces human interaction in all its diversity.

A number of available inservice training packs seek to address issues in discipline and behaviour management and to provide a foundation for organizers and participants to achieve the following:

• raise awareness of the conceptual and definitional issues to do with disruptive, maladaptive, non-compliant behaviour, and critically examine terms like 'maladjustment';

- acquire knowledge of developments in theory, provision, research, survey evidence, treatment methods;
- develop personal and professional skills to deal with, and respond to, behaviour difficulties and to be enabled to plan and carry out individual and group programmes, as well as to revise school policy.

The packs and booklets cited below combine theory with practice. Some emphasize the conceptual and knowledge base, others explicitly focus on direct 'hands on' skills acquisition and aim to provide frameworks and strategies for responding to identified problems in order to effect measurable change in behaviour and/or to enhance learning competence. We have not included costs of materials as prices quickly become out of date.

Part A - A selective, annotated review of resources

Ainscow, M and Muncey, J (1985) *Special Needs Action Programme (SNAP).* **Drake Educational Associates: Cardiff.**

Purpose:
A series of self-contained modular courses, first designed as a whole-school inservice and teacher support service for use in Coventry primary schools, but now extended to secondary schools.

Contents:
Comprised of audio-visual programmes, tutors' and workshop members' guides and record keeping approaches.

A range of special needs is catered for within the SNAP system as a whole. Of particular relevance to learning and behaviour management is Module 6 'Problem behaviour in the primary school' which looks at problem definition, management, organisation and support within schools, and classroom management.

Chisholm, B, Kearney, D, Knight, G, Little, H, Morris, S and Tweddle, D (1986) *Preventive Approaches to Disruption (PAD),* **Macmillan: Basingstoke. Now available from NFER-Nelson.**

Purpose:
Workshop-based INSET materials for teachers in secondary schools.

Contents:
Consists of six units and an accompanying video:
    1. using PAD in schools;
    2. non-verbal communication;
    3. lesson organisation;

4. management of pupils;
5. observation guides;
6. developing teaching skills.

Flexibility delivered by way of 'contacted' workshop INSET sessions, intended to be 'tailored' to individual schools' needs, following discussions between course leader and school.

Dawson, R (ed. in association with Barnsley LEA) (1985) *The Teacher Information Pack (TIPS)* **NFER-Nelson: Windsor.**

Purpose:
Boxed resource packs which give teachers and other professionals ready access to concise, useful and practical information on a wide range of educational topics and concerns. One of the five main areas is Behaviour, including disruption, solvent and drug abuse, anxiety, bullying and swearing.

Contents:
The TIPS Primary Pack - this includes 125 booklets; a Teacher's Guide, and a Support Services' Guide which lists local and national support agencies.

The TIPS Secondary Pack - includes 125 booklets from the primary pack plus an additional 10 secondary school booklets; 5 copies of the Secondary School User's Guide; a Special Needs Co-ordinator's Guide, and a pad of 25 photocopiable Diagnostic Record Sheets.

One of the cards presented is entitled, 'Problem-solving approach for changing behaviour'. This consists of discussion and suggestions for activities and further reading. Other units include: observation and recording; classroom organisation; sociometry; behaviour and modification.

Galvin, P, Mercer, S, and Costa, P (1990) *Building a Better Behaved School,* **Longman: Harlow.**

Purpose:
A development manual for primary schools (in ring-binder format) for school based INSET.

Contents:
A three-tier model of approaches to behaviour management. Nine units: whole-school focus:
1. Effective school;
2. School reviews;

44

3. Positive school discipline plans;
4. Working with parents;
5. Curriculum organisation and behaviour management: group/class focus;
6. Preventive classroom management;
7. Rules, praise, ignore;
8. Heavyweight strategies for the classroom;
9. Working with individuals.

The package allows for optional entry points (doesn't need to be sequentially worked through) depending on priorities. Additional resources include; printed sheets, activities, and a sample outline on truanting.

Grunsell, R (1985) *Finding Answers to Disruption: Discussion Exercises for Secondary Teachers,* **Longman: Harlow.**

Purpose:
Specific exercises designed for secondary teachers to provide teacher groups with structured exercises on various aspects of disruption. To help groups work together to formulate their own solutions to problems with which they are confronted.

Contents:
User notes, including how to use the materials, finding priority issues, etc. Discussion materials are divided into several parts:
1. defining the problem;
2. finding a basis for action;
3. improving things for teachers/pupils;
4. attention seeking behaviour;
5. the 'difficult' class;
6. use of checklists;
7. asking for support.

Each part consists of 20-plus exercises outlined precisely in terms of time/content/etc. and covering issues such as:

- authority;
- stress;
- dealing with confrontation.

These materials are particularly good for school-focused or teacher-focused INSET work. They analyse needs, raise awareness of issues and are useful for staff/group building. They DO NOT provide solutions but only provide ways of exploring problem areas as a group exercise.

Hanko, G (1990) *Special Needs in Ordinary Classrooms,* (2nd edition) Simon and Schuster: London.

Purpose:
The author sees the principle of this book as a response to the growing interest in the possibilities, principles and practices of school-based support and training. There is a growing advocacy that professionals with expertise in SEN should be involved in systematic work with teachers in order to extend and enhance teachers' own skills and knowledge regarding children with emotional and behavioural difficulties in their classrooms. Gerda Hanko explores the underlying principles, issues, functions and approaches in setting up and running teacher support groups.

Contents:
Part One - case studies are used to demonstrate the consultancy model in action. Problems are seen to be explored collaboratively, the consultant acting as a facilitator and the group sharing and generating their own solutions.

Part Two - explores the issues, functions and approaches which underpin her model.

Part Three - provides detailed discussion regarding the setting up of teacher support groups in a variety of settings. The roles and tasks are explored together with the use of internal or external consultants. Opportunities and obstacles are addressed.

Hertfordshire LEA (February 1992) *Behaviour Matters,* and *Management of Pupil Behaviour* (1991). Modules 1-4 (one ring-bound volume), and 5-9 (one ring-bound volume), County Hall, Hertford.

Purpose:
a. *Management of Pupil Behaviour* - the two volumes comprise a training pack for teachers.

Contents:
There are eight overlapping modules in the management of pupil behaviour designed to be used over six sessions by groups of staff. The eight modules are: classroom management; curriculum; rules; communication skills; parents; bullying and truancy; conflict and stress-management; self-esteem.

b. *Behaviour Matters* - this ring-bound pack follows on from the modules and is designed to assist schools to develop their own whole-school policies on discipline and behaviour.

Contents:
The set of materials comprises stimulus for staff to work together to create policy. It encourages staff to consider: values and principles; analyse classroom and out-of-classroom contexts; child abuse and child protection; bullying and harassment; playtimes and dinnertimes; working with parents; strategies for individuals; organisation of teaching and learning; communication.

Jolly, M and McNamara, E (1991) *Towards Better Behaviour* - available from 7 Quinton Close, Ainsdale, Merseyside PR8 2JD.

Purpose:
This behaviourally-based resource pack is aimed at the assessment and analysis of pupil problem behaviour.

Contents:
The pack comprises:
- the pupil management checklist;
- the classroom situation checklist;
- the pupil behaviour schedule;
- the off-task behaviour analysis schedule;
- an 86-page manual.

Luton, K, Booth, G, Leadbetter, J, Tee, G, and Wallace, F, (1992) *Positive Strategies for Behaviour Management,* NFER-Nelson: Windsor.

Purpose:
This is a behaviourally-based training pack for primary teachers. It sets out a practical course of action for the development of a whole school policy. It is derived from good practice in schools and involves non-teaching staff, parents and governors as well as teachers and pupils.

Contents:
The pack takes the form of a course leader's handbook which covers: Introduction; Rules and Reinforcement; School Organisation; Parents and the Community; Support for Teachers; Producing a Behaviour Management Policy. Each unit includes photocopyable sheets; handouts and ready made OHP transparencies.

Lund, R et al (1992) *Behaviour Matters,* **Hertfordshire LEA. Available from County Hall, Hertford.**

Purpose:
This is a training pack aimed at primary schools.

Contents:
Set out in a ring-binder, the pack contains a number of units including supporting exercises and reference lists. The areas covered are:
- keeping safe;
- playtimes and dinner times;
- involving parents;
- strategies for individuals;
- organisation of teaching and learning;
- communication.

McGuire, J (1988) *The Isolated Withdrawn and Anxious Child,* **NFER-Nelson: Windsor.**

Purpose:
Identification and assessment for parents, teachers, EPs, other professionals.

Contents:
1. development trends;
2. causes;
3. severe disorders;
4. helping children with emotional problems;
5. day-care provision;
6. identification problems;
7. managing transition;
8. management in group settings.

Maines, B and Robinson, G (1988) *A Bag of Tricks,* **Lame Duck Publishing, 10 South Terrace, Redland, Bristol, BS6 6TG.**

Purpose:
A staff development pack. It lasts for at least one day's INSET or for five after-school sessions.

Contents:
An ideas and work book with photocopiable information sheets and worksheets.

McLean, A (1993), *Promoting Positive Behaviour,* **Jordanhill College of Education. ISBN 1 85098 0 K31.**

Purpose:
This is a package for trainers to use with teachers. It provides a stimulus and structure which will encourage the discussion of a range of issues and approaches to promoting positive behaviour.

Contents:
There are two packs: one for primary schools, and one for secondary. In each, twelve 90 minute sessions are planned. All the necessary materials for the activities are provided: a group leader's book; a video, and photocopy master sheets. Suggestions for follow-up activities are also included.

The key assumptions are that teachers' behaviour has a great influence on pupils' behaviour, also that positive group management can be described, practised and acquired. Issues covered include;

- school ethos;
- conveying authority;
- classroom climate;
- picking up signals;
- rules, rewards and punishments;
- defusing confrontations;
- stopping misbehaviour;
- minimising dead time.

This is a well thought out programme for preventing disruption on the classroom.

Munro, A, Manthei, R, and Small, J (1989) *Counselling: The Skills of Problem-Solving,* **Routledge: London.**

Purpose:
The authors state that this book is for counsellors working in various settings (educational, vocational, medical and social) and those offering training courses to counsellors. The authors all practice counselling in New Zealand.

Contents:
Using a problem-solving approach:
- problem definition;
- goal selection;
- strategy selection;
- implementation of strategy;
- evaluation.

The authors demonstrate the skills involved in helping other solve their problems. The first half of the book develops the above model, the second half offers chapters on: A Maori perspective, family counselling, consultation and developing competence.

This book is direct and comprehensive. Each chapter contains theoretical discussion and practical exercises (for individual pairs and group work) which reflect theory and raise self-awareness, and enhance counselling skills.

NFER-Nelson (1988) *Professional Learning Resources,* **NFER-Nelson: Windsor.**

Consists of three large binders/packs, each comprising of:
- course leaders' in-service planning instructions;
- ready-made overhead projector transparencies;
- tasks and discussion activities;
- course manuals for organisers and participants;
- handouts which may be photocopied.

Purpose:
(In ring-binder format) Inservice training with multi-disciplinary groups. Introduction to therapeutic techniques and skills with case examples and exercises.

Contents:
Contents of units:
- Douglas, J. (Ed) *Emotional and Behavioural Problems in Young Children: a multidisciplinary approach to identification and management* - Includes: sleep disturbance, feeding problems, sexual abuse, surviving marital breakdown, anti-social behaviour, the isolated, withdrawn and anxious child.

- Monk, E. (Ed) *Emotional and Behavioural Problems in Adolescence: a multidisciplinary approach to identification and management* - Includes: normal development, substance abuse, eating disorders, sexuality and sexual abuse, working with parents, marital breakdown, aggressive and disruptive behaviour.

- Smith, J. and Bryans, T. (Eds) *Issues in Statementing Children with Emotional and Behavioural Problems - a multidisciplinary approach* - Includes: the 1981 Education Act, nature of the problems, teacher's role, the health contribution, the role of the psychologist, the administrator, social services, the parent's contribution, special issues.

Each unit is independent, with course leader notes, exercises using case studies and OHTs included.

Northumberland Education Department (1991) (joint project by educational psychologists, teachers and advisers) *Let's Get On* **(Improving Social Skills) (2nd edition). Enquiries: 0670 519959**

Purpose:
Improving social skills. Improving pupils'/teachers' learning skills. Advocating tolerance of others and self. Improving schools' armoury of responses to difficult pupils and pupils with difficulties.

Contents:
Communicating effectively; Dealing with anxiety; Establishing and maintaining relationships; Keeping out of trouble; Dealing with aggressive behaviour; Being positive about yourself and others; Becoming more assertive.

This is a package of materials for various groups to work through and provides 'pupils'-guide' to behaving well, emphasising appropriate delivery of rewards. Delivery is by interactive role play activities, as well as prepared discussion materials.

OPTIS: Training guides for teachers and non-teaching staff working with pupils with special educational needs. Module 2 for teachers, covers emotional and behavioural problems. Available from: Cricket Road Centre, Oxford OX4 3DW

Purpose:
To examine strategies and develop skills.

Contents:
Topics include: assessment, identification, social factors, curriculum implications, managing behaviour in the classroom, policy. *Working Together* materials are directed at non-teaching staff and includes a section on 'Emotional and Behavioural Difficulties' to assist staff to 'develop skills needed to help pupils form meaningful relationships, support pupils and understand parents' anxieties'.

NB. OPTIS training offers the possibility of certification, via the University of the West of England.

Oxford Brookes University, (in association with the Directorate of Education Advisory Service, London Borough of Bexley) (1990) *Discipline in Schools; The Elton Report: a study pack.*

Purpose:
To familiarise school staff with the content of The Elton Report and encourage the development of new school policies.

Contents:
One video and loose leaf file, divided into ten sections, each containing information and suggested activities to study specific issues deriving from the Elton Report.

The loose leaf format allows for a flexible use of materials, but it is suggested that separate groups study specific sections and issues therein, feeding back within the context of a plenary session.

The sections are:
- Ancillaries and supervision of free time;
- Classroom management;
- Curriculum delivery;
- Buildings and environment;
- Pastoral systems;
- Leadership and management;
- Parental contact and involvement;
- Additional subsections involving organisation of whole material.

Pickles, T (1992) *Dealing with Disaffection.* **A practical response to school related issues. Longman: Harlow.**

Purpose:
A practical training manual to help teachers to reduce pupil disruption, truancy and disaffection.

Contents:
The materials include exercises and worksheets.

Reid, K (Ed) (1989) *Helping Troubled Pupils in Secondary School,* **Volumes 1 and 2, Simon and Schuster: London.**

Purpose:
Deals with the personality, behaviour and emotional problems of pupils in the secondary school.

Contents:
Volume 1 - social, psychological and professional issues.
Volume 2 - managerial topics, non-attenders, the combined role of home and school.

Robertson, J (1990) (2nd edition) *Effective Classroom Control,* Hodder and Stoughton: London.

Purpose:
For teachers - promotion of classroom management skills.

Contents:
1. Expressing authority;
2. Nature of authority;
3. Establishing authority;
4. Conveying enthusiasm;
5. Analysing unwanted behaviour;
6. Dealing with unwanted behaviour;
7. The way ahead.

Rogers, B (1991) *You know the fair rule.* Strategies for making the hard job of discipline in school easier. Longman: Harlow.

Purpose:
This book examines the realities of dealing with troublesome behaviour and aims to 'make a hard job easy'.

Contents:
The book provides a wide range of strategies and practical skills aimed to help new and experienced teachers.

Sprick, R (1981) *The Solution Book: a guide to classroom discipline,* Science Research Associates: Henley on Thames.

Purpose:
Aimed at teachers, psychologists and other professionals involved in various problematic situations.

Contents:
A large ring-bound manual, originally prepared in USA, consisting of three sections. The first section consists of nine topic areas:
1. Getting started;
2. Effective reinforcement;
3. Effective punishment;
4. Ignoring misbehaviour and setting goals for behaviour;

5. Increasing positive interactions and improving student's self concept;
6. Small group instruction and independent seatwork;
7. Techniques, e.g. peer tutoring, individualized instruction, learning centres, group projects;
8. Establishing a discipline plan;
9. Survival skills for teachers.

The second section comprises 100 solution sheets, each presenting a short case study and suggesting a plan for solving behaviour and learning problems; and the final section contains materials that may be reproduced.

Stone, L (1992) (Second Edition) *Managing Difficult Children in School,* **Simon and Schuster: London.**

Purpose:
Provides down-to-earth advice on a variety of difficult situations in mainstream schools, Years 7 - 11.

Contents:
Examines the effect of school, class and home management on children's behaviour. Deals with problems of stress, rejection, fear and anxiety.

Stow, L M, Stringer, P H Hibbert, K A, and Powell, J, *Understanding and Manging Difficult Behaviour: Establishing Staff Support Groups - Training Manuals* **(1992), Newcastle-upon-Tyne Educational Psychology Service. Further details from: Educational Psychology Service, East View, Ayton Street, Newcastle-upon-Tyne, NE6 2DB.**

Purpose:
To help teachers to set up their own staff development groups, also to encourage schools to create a supportive learning environment. The aim is to allow teachers to experience the extent to which they can contribute to each other's effectiveness by sharing their professional expertise.

Contents:
There are three manuals originally designed to accompany a three day course. Two separate but interlinked Training Manuals, for facilitators and tutors, contain the information and workshop activities necessary for setting-up collaborative staff development groups. Having completed these, course members can then use the third manual to introduce the training programme in their own schools.

Strathclyde Department of Education (1988) *Preventing Disruption: A Classroom Management approach.* **Co-ordinator: Alan McLean, Deputy Principal Psychologist.**

Purpose:
To provide the basis of any staff development exercise dealing with pupil/classroom management, and to develop the ability to reflect or/and evaluate one's own teaching practice.

Contents:
Seven core units:
1. Lesson Organisation;
2. Rules and Routines;
3. Conveying Authority;
4. Avoiding Confrontation;
5. Rewards and Punishments;
6. Classroom Climate and School Ethos;
7. Stress Management.

Each unit comprises group leader materials, study notes, activity sheets. There are three accompanying videos. Units are to be delivered systematically in the order given - each unit to be in a single block of one hour minimum. The sessions use group discussion, individual/paired activities, role play/simulation, and video based exercises.

Has good back-up sheets to support the main booklets, e.g. prepared OHTs, and provides a thorough overview of basic teaching skills in the classroom.

Watkins, C. and Wagner, P. (1987) *School Discipline: A whole school practical approach,* **Basil Blackwell: Oxford. Now available from Simon and Schuster.**

Purpose:
'To empower teachers in their understanding of indiscipline and their response to it'.

Contents:
This book takes an interactionist, systems perspective, with an emphasis on equal opportunities.

Wheldall, K. (Ed) (1987) *The Behaviourist in the Classroom,* **Educational Review: University of Birmingham.**

Purpose:
For EPs and teachers - behavioural techniques for assessment and management.

Contents:
1. Discussions of behavioural techniques;
2. Applications in secondary schools;
3. Applications at home;
4. Applications in primary schools;
5. Applications in a special school;
6. Training teachers to use BATPACK;
7. Ethical issues.

Wheldall, K. and Merritt, F. (1984) *The Behavioural Approach to Teaching Package (BATPACK),* **University of Birmingham and Positive Products.**

Purpose:
The package is aimed at primary school teachers (with a specific target of involving schools' headteachers) in a series of 'skill acquisition' sessions.

Contents:
The course is run by an 'accredited course tutor', who has attended a prescribed course of training, using a scripted manual for six sessions, focusing on:
- identifying troublesome behaviour;
- an overview of the behavioural approach to teaching;
- focusing on good behaviour; practicing positives;
- achieving the right classroom setting;
- dealing with more troublesome behaviour.

The emphasis is on changing teacher's behaviour via a series of 'workshop/video/exercise/homework activities', using pupils' responses (behaviours) as a measure of this effect. The simple 'homework' activities allow an opportunity to integrate an INSET training session with the ongoing teaching experience of the course participants. A more recently published secondary phase version, BATSAC, is also available.

Wiltshire Education Department (Psychological and Advisory Service) (1989) *Wiltshire Adjustment Support Preparation (WASP).*

Purpose:
To provide a programme of training for support (behaviour) teachers on pupil adjustment problems and issues. The focus is on the provision of support to classroom teachers in its broadest context, rather than on basic teaching skills and techniques, which constitute good classroom management.

Contents:
Eleven units which should be delivered in the order given. They give a comprehensive guide through the relevant issues - provision, identification and assessment, intervention and the organisation and politics of schools. Additionally, issues to do with self-organisation and stress are addressed, and a variety of techniques for the active involvement of participants is used.

Part B - Bullying: Resources, training, advice, packs, videos, organisations (see also references in Section 2)

A.B.C. (Anti-Bullying Campaign) *Schools Pack.* 18 Elmgage Gardens, Edgware, Middlesex HA8 9RT.

Besag, V. (1989) *Bullying and Victims in Schools.* Open University Press: Milton Keynes.

Besag, V. *We don't have bullies here.* Ring-binder from 57 Manor House Road, Jesmond, Newcastle-upon-Tyne NE2 2LY.

Brock, E. (1992) *A Positive Approach to Bullying.* INSET Pack. Longman: Harlow.

Casdagli, O. (1990) *Only Playing, Miss.* (Play/Workshop) Trentham Books: Stoke-on-Trent. (also on video)

Elliott, M. (1991) *Stop Bullying.* KIDSCAPE, World Trade Centre, Europe House, London E1 9AA.

Essex LEA (West Essex Learning Support Service) *A Positive Approach to Bullying.* A4 Pack - also video and audiotape.

Humberside LEA/EPs (1991) *The Prevention of School-based Bullying - a whole-school approach.* Distance learning pack.

Jewers, T (1993) *Hands on Bullying,* Tony Jewers Productions, 4 Greystones Close, Colchester, Essex, CO3 4RQ.

- video tape suitable for pupils in the 8 - 18 age range.

KIDSCAPE, World Trade Centre, Europe House, London E1 9AA, (books, booklets, training, advice). *No Blame and Michael's Story,* video and INSET book.

Stamp out Bullying (1991) Video and handbook. Both from Lame Duck Publishing, 10 South Terrace, Bristol, BS6 6TG.

SCRE (Scottish Council for Research in Education) *Action against Bullying.* Pack available from 15 St. John Street, Edinburgh.

Sheffield University. Bullying Projects (DES/DFE funded) (Smith, Thomson, et al), produces papers and newsletters, Psychology Department, Sheffield University, Sheffield S10 2TN.

Skinner, A. (1992) *Bullying: an annotated bibliography of literature and resources.* Youth Work Press: Leicester (*strongly recommended, as it contains sections on: The Evidence; Research; Positive approaches; Resources; Support organisations and helplines).

Tattum, D (1993) *Cycle of Violence,* Drake Educational Associates: Cardiff.

- video tape accompanied by teacher's notes.

ON CHILD ABUSE/CHILD SEXUAL ABUSE - See references in Section 2, also:

Materials by KIDSCAPE (address in previous section)

Brock, E. (1992) *Child Abuse and the Schools' Response.* Longman: Harlow.

Purpose:
This is a one-day INSET pack, aimed at school personnel, combining giving information, group work and other exercises designed to increase awareness and develop skills.

Contents:
Background to and definition of child abuse; signs; referral; dealing with disclosure; school procedures; issues.

Appendices

LEARNING-DESCRIPTION OBSERVATION SHEET

Purpose

This observation sheet consists of paired items. Both statements in each pair are contrasting descriptions of the child's learning behaviour in the classroom and in school.

The sheet is designed to help the teacher examine in some detail facets of the child's behaviour in these areas. It is not a test, as with a pass or fail, but provides an opportunity for the teacher to observe the child's positive and negative (worrying) behaviour.

Instructions

The 15 paired statements describe the child's behaviour in learning situations. Please read each pair of statements carefully and write the answer to each question as accurately and briefly as possible.

Examples

In which learning situation does the child:
9. Show concentration?   *Show distractibility?*

Written responses might be:
infant age
   In music and movement   In story time, writing
   Sand and water play

junior age
   In English lessons   In maths

secondary age
   In activity-based lessons   In lessons requiring him/her
                                   to read

Action

From these observations and recordings should emerge a picture of the child's coping strategies as well as problem areas. This could be the baseline for action on the part of the teacher in terms of:

activity choices, handling style, promotion or restriction of contact with other children, organisation matters such as a change of seating arrangements, further enquiries into the child's home circumstances, further assessment, referral to support agencies.

Appendix 1b

LEARNING-DESCRIPTION OBSERVATION SHEET

Name ....Boy/Girl (tick) Date of birth.................................

Class teacher...................................... Date of completion ....

Completed by.................................... Designation.................................

In which learning situation does the child:

1. Show curiosity?   Lack curiosity?

2. Listen to verbal instructions?   Not listen to verbal instructions?

3. Show interest?   Lack interest?

4. Understand instructions?   Fail to understand instructions?

5. Seem settled?   Seem restless, unsettled?

6. Co-operate?   Show hostility?

7. Give impression of being alert?   Give impression of being dull?

8. Attend to the task?   Not attend to the task?

9. Show concentration?   Show distractibility?

10. Instigate learning?   Show passivity?

11. Show goal directed behaviour?   Show aimless, inconsequential behaviour?

12. Enjoy doing the set tasks?   Avoid doing the set tasks?

13. Understand the purpose of tasks?   Seem unable to understand the purposes of tasks?

14. Show reflective learning behaviour? Show impulsive learning behaviour?

15. Complete set work?   Seldom produce work?

This page may be copied.

Appendix 2a

PERSONAL-DESCRIPTIVE OBSERVATION SHEET

Purpose
This observation sheet consists of paired items. Both statements in each pair are contrasting descriptions of the child's social and emotional behaviour in the classroom and school, with other children and adults.

The sheet is designed to help the teacher examine in some detail facets of the child's behaviour in these areas. It is not a test, as with a pass or fail, but provides an opportunity for the teacher to observe the child's positive and negative behaviour.

Instructions
The 18 paired statements fall into three categories. There are six peer group items, eight self items, and four adult interaction items.

Examples
In which situation does the child:
1. *Co-operate with other children?*   *Fail to co-operate with other children?*

Written responses might be:
infant age

| When supervised | Doing Lego |
| In small supervised groups | In the playground at mealtimes |

junior age

| In drama lessons | In PE |
| | In the playground |

secondary age

| When task is explained to him/her directly | When s/he does not understand the task |

Action
From these observations and recordings should emerge a picture of the child's coping strategies as well as problem areas. This could be the baseline for action on the part of the teacher in terms of:

activity choices, handling style, promotion or restriction of contact with other children, organisation matters such as a change of seating arrangements, further enquiries into the child's home circumstances, further diagnostic assessment, referral to support agencies.

Appendix 2b

PERSONAL-DESCRIPTIVE OBSERVATION SHEET

Name ....Boy/Girl (tick) Date of birth................................

Class teacher...................................... Date of completion.....................

Completed by................................. Designation................................

In which situation does the child:

1. Co-operate with other children?(P)
   (P) Fail to co-operate with other children?

2. Settle in a small group?(P)
   (P) Disrupt a small group?

3. Accept other children's leadership?(P)
   (P) Bully or provoke confrontation?

4. Seek out other children?(P)
   (P) Avoid other children?

5. Seem popular with other children?(P)
   (P) Seem unpopular with other children?

6. Instigate play with other children?(P)
   (P) Passively accept other children's suggestions?

7. Show equable behaviour?(S)
   (S) Seem volatile and upset?

8. Seem outgoing?(S)
   (S) Become withdrawn?

9. Seem self-reliant?(S)
   (S) Seem dependent on others?

10. Seem alert?(S)
    (S) Seem tired and listless?

11. Seem happiest?(S)
    (S) Seem most unhappy?

12. Show social reflectivity?(S)
    (S) Show social impulsivity?

13. Show serene behaviour?(S)
    (S) Show hyperactive, restless behaviour?

14. Seem relaxed, at ease?(S)
    (S) Seem overcontrolled, tense?

15. Fit in with classroom routine?(A)
    (A) Require constant reprimands?

16. Carry out teacher requests?(A)
    (A) Refuse to co-operate with teacher?

17. Seem amenable to, and accepting of adult control?(A)
    (A) Seem impervious to adult control?

18. Accept responsibilities?(A)
    (A) Avoid responsibilities?

Key to code letters: (P) Peer group contact (S) Self   (A) Adult interaction

This page may be copied.